FOSTER PARENT & SUBSTITUTE TEACHER: WORLD'S GREATEST JOBS

Managing Children With Difficult Behaviors

LOIS SIMMONS

The author acknowledges and is grateful to Virginia Holloway for permission to
use her published article "Foster Care Opens Future for Kids"

Inquiries and Book Orders should be addressed to:

 Great Writers Media

Great Writers Media
Email: info@greatwritersmedia.com
Phone: 877-600-5469

ISBN: 978-1-960939-58-6 (sc)
ISBN: 978-1-960939-59-3 (ebk)

ACKNOWLEDGEMENT

Thank God for directing my path and sharpening my skills, enabling me to do what I do for others. I, also, express my gratitude to all my children, Erika, Christopher and Kimberly who assisted me in the care of other people's children by furnishing me necessary information, teaching me how to use the Internet and just doing whatever I needed them to do to help the process along. I thank my grandchildren, Jasmyn, Kaylan, Terry, Autumn, Ambria, and Aaron for sharing me with the children I've cared for. They would always tell the new children what I liked and didn't like to try to keep the children out of trouble and to keep peace in the house, although it didn't work all the time. They would also tell me when the children got out of line and did something they were told not to do. They are terrific examples of how they were trained. I am so fortunate to have them all!

DEDICATION

I dedicate this book to Ms. "B" (Bernice Johnson), one of my closest friends and confidants. She was a true friend to everyone who knew her. She lived 70+ years and spent her life dealing with other people's children. She showed much love by taking care of, teaching and guiding children. She loved family gatherings. She made it a passion to remember everybody's birthday like no one I ever knew. She would call or send a portion of whatever she had to adults and children alike, near and afar off. She was love personified. I miss our times together.

CONTENTS

Acknowledgement...3

Dedication 5

Foreword...9

Two States Of Mind..17

Get To Know Your Opponent 21

Care, Choices, Consequences And Consistency.............26

The Need To Manipulate And Control...........................31

Support Groups..37

The Matter of Finances..39

Road Map To Success 41

Substitute Teacher: Another Lovely World....................50

A Substitute Teacher's Day 58

Making Ready For The Challenge 60

Both Jobs Propelled Me Forward....................................64

FOREWORD

Foster parents and substitute teachers just get no respect. So, how can I think these are two of the world's greatest jobs? They are, if you learn how to master them. After you've learned to master them, you might even develop a passion for them and not want to do any other kind of work. I know that everyone who reads the title of this book will think I've lost my mind. I had to lose what was left of my mind in order to renew my mind to truth and facts. I had to have spiritual guidance to get me to the point of knowing I needed help in what I was trying to do. As long as I tried to do things the way I thought they should work, the more I failed. Not many people are willing to take on the position of a foster parent or a substitute teacher. There is no scarcity in jobs fostering children and if you can find schools with behavior problems, finding a substitute position is not a problem. There is always a need for both. Some of these positions only require a high school education and a state license in various places. Some places require a little college to substitute. If you work with children today, a background check will be required. My best advice to anyone who would like to pursue this opportunity is not to do it just to get paid. You must have a desire or some inner spirit prompting you to really want to help children or you will make your life miserable. I will walk you through my experiences in which

I hope you will find that through it all, I've learned to enjoy what I do. I manage children with difficult behavior with what I call the 4-C's: Care, Choices, Consequences, and Consistency. Fostering and substituting are very challenging experiences. I am not one to be afraid of a challenge. You won't succeed if you have fear. In your best heart, always know that you want what is best for the children and that you want to help them reach for something far greater than their present circumstances. You need to know these things before you make the decision to plunge into a situation that may prove to not be good for you or a child. You will be held spiritually accountable for what happens to a child entrusted in your care. So, if you have any doubts about anything, find someone you trust to give good advice and ask questions, do research, and examine yourself and your motives for doing it, as well as the motives of others. If you have a family, you must by all means put them first and know that they will be able to handle situations involving what they could view as an intruder coming to take their place. After all, who wants to share their parents with someone they don't even know. In fostering someone else's child, you must always be mindful of the effect a seemingly innocent being could have on your life or the lives of other members in your family. This could usher in the jealousy beast on both sides. Make no decision without prayer. Wait and see if you get direction from God to foster or sub children. This is my advice to you. I didn't follow any of this advice because I didn't have it. That's why it took a long time for me to begin to learn my lessons. I went through many foster children before I finally figured out why the disruptions came. This was the way for the children, who didn't want to obey you in the first place, to get to go to another home. They would like to find a place where they can take over and rule. Children don't under-stand how becoming structured and stable is good for them. We can't allow them to continue the path of running away, because they're not going anywhere or learning anything. They're only prolonging the inevitable. We must commit to having staying power for the sake of the child, especially if that child has no family to go to. But I am grateful to God that He kept me powered-up through it all and He is there to help me. I wouldn't be where I am without Him.

This is where I need to see if you're spiritually developed enough to know and understand the God kind of love, which is Agape, unconditional love and if you are able to practice it on others. This will be your greatest asset and greatest need. If you possess this kind of love, you will be able to remain steadfast and unmovable. Love is the most important attribute you can share with a child. Let LOVE be your guide. Either one of these endeavors could end up being the most rewarding challenge of your life or your worst nightmare, because these children come to you with so much baggage. So, if you're carrying around a lot of your own baggage, consider putting this challenge on hold until you get your act together. You will be doing God and a child a disservice to take on this responsibility just to be compensated. If you're not ready yet, WAIT! If compensation is not your main reason for doing it and you're ready, let the challenges begin! Let me advise you now to show strength and not weakness. Show that you are in command over your household and your own children, if you have them. The less information the children know about you, the less number of your buttons they'll be able to push. They have trained themselves to push your buttons. Push your buttons mean "I get on your nerves until you give me what I want". You must place yourself in a listening mode at all times. That's what the children do. When your inner spirit tells you something is up with your children, don't ignore it. Don't brush away that feeling. There usually is something going on. Start asking questions and listening and asking more questions. Soon, you'll discover that something was going on. As mothers, God gives us this innate ability to just know things. Children know that we have something, but they just don't quite know what it is or how to explain it. I like to tell them they're not getting by me; I've got eyes everywhere. With God, this is true, God has eyes everywhere! Don't you just love it? They will look at you like something is wrong with you and that's just where you want them. Always keep them not knowing what you might do. Just show up at their school sometimes, when they least expect it. Kids keep me young in mind. I love them and I love having them around. It's like I'm in school, always learning some new game they want to play. It's a real challenge and I love it. I signed on Facebook, one of the social networking sites on the Internet and my oldest grand-daughter called me by phone, in disbelief and said, "Nana, you're on Facebook, I accepted you as my friend". She said she had to call her friends and tell them, "you better watch what you say on Facebook, cause my Nana's on there now!" I tell them all that they don't ever know when or where I might show up! But hear me, my words are to inspire, inform and to motivate you. They're not to discourage you in any way. When I started fostering, I didn't have a clue. I had a nephew who my mother adopted because his mother didn't want him. He was my oldest brother's child. He was two weeks old when my mother got him. He won my mother's heart and of course we all loved him. My mother was able to do more financially for him at the time, than she could ever do for my youngest brother or me. Even surrounded by love as he grew up, I could never understand why this child exhibited so many problems. He could have very well been on drugs. I don't know if that was the case. He had difficulties obeying at home and at my mama's house, you weren't going to just do any-thing you wanted to do, when you wanted to do it. So, he thought he could go out and stay past curfew. He came home one night and my mother had the door locked and chained. He wasn't going to get in her house. She finally had to let go of him and allow God to deal with him. It broke her heart, but she felt she had no choice. He would go from home to home, carrying around his belongings in a big black plastic bag. He would stay a day or two, here or there with friends. He was a very likeable young man and people did try to help him. He even stayed with me a few times. He was a very intelligent person. He only finished high school, but he would end up with the best of jobs right out of high school, like an apprenticeship to be an electrician and got paid well for it. He would never keep the jobs. One other thing that added to his problem was getting to know his mother and finding out earlier that she had kept a son from another relationship. It made him wonder why she gave him away. He always questioned why she gave him away.

I was a telephone operator at Veterans Hospital, working the midnight shift one night, when the Administrative Officer of the Day (AOD) came down with two policemen to inform me that my brother/nephew had been shot and killed in Atlanta, Georgia. He had broken up from a bad relationship, accepted Jesus as his Savior and was making a transition to a new life when he was shot and killed by an ex-girlfriend. The good news was that he was saved at the time of his death, but I didn't have peace with his death until God revealed to me that my brother/nephew was never going to be able to get over the fact that his mother gave him away. That was the only thing that made sense to me. I could accept his death when I knew and understood that fact. That's when I decided I wanted to reach out and help someone else's child. A friend that I worked with as a telephone operator told me that she had been a foster parent at one time. She told me that you get paid for it and that she was about to do it again. She wanted me to attend classes with her because she was going to a new agency and she didn't want to do it alone. I thought, well I could use more income. I never knew this type of job existed. I had lost my nephew a few months prior to this. I did a lot of thinking about whether I should do this. I kept thinking how I couldn't help my nephew with his problems; maybe I could help someone else's child. I said yes to her and she picked up the paperwork for the training and afterwards decided she wasn't going to do it right then. I completed the training and have successfully worked with three Birmingham agencies since 1998. There are hundreds of our children in foster care. The list grows longer each day. I didn't have any experience at all doing this, so please consider helping children today! I believe you can master the art of fostering. Join me. I always say, Lord, just let me help one and He does. To Him Be The GLORY!!!

TWO STATES OF MIND

TWO STATES OF MIND

After much prayer and consideration, you've decided to take the plunge and bring a child into your home. I commend you on your decision. I think it's a great and wonderful thing you're doing, giving of your life this way. I'm assuming you have a strong belief system to take on this task, especially if you are a single parent. If you don't have a strong belief system, you may have just made a sad mistake. But, if you plan to be in it for the long haul, then you are just what a child needs. Let's first walk you through your thoughts as you prepare to meet this new addition to the family. At first, you're nervous and not knowing what to expect because this is a total stranger coming to live in your home. I feel as if all children are therapeutic and possess the same characteristics. The difference is, foster children rarely is trained up in the way they should go and by the time you get them, they don't want to be trained, they want to train you. So, you're wondering how bad the situation could be. It's just a child. You're thinking, I'm a good person, inviting this child into my home to help care for him/her. They will really like me because I'm going to treat them as if they are my very own. Stop!!! Stop!!! Reality check! The child has been through so many traumas and disappointments in his life, he doesn't care about any of the things you're thinking or feeling. Because of this, don't expect the child to come in smiling like you're buddies. Not going to happen! They are usually reserved and standoffish. They are quiet and waiting on you to carry the conversation. The child is sizing you up and looking around your place to see what might be desirable. So, if you have anything valuable, you might want to remove the temptation before he/she arrives. All the children won't steal from you, but some will and you should be aware of this. Some of them have deep-seated problems and will take anything not nailed down. They are in the system and around other children in the system that steals as a way to survive or take things they aren't able to get otherwise. Locked doors and keys work well for these type situations. They will have some kind of problem that you aren't aware of and you will learn about it as you live with them. As you put your best foot forward, being friendly and accommodating to the child and social worker, the child is watching and listening intently at you. The child is listening for phrases you might say to give him a clue as to what it is going to be like living with you. If you will pay attention, the child will never do much talking about himself and if he does start to talk to you, it will be mostly questions trying to figure out what kind of rules you have or if you will take him places he/she wants to go. The child wants to know how much he/she will have to put up with and what kind of buttons he/she will need to push in order to get another home if things don't turn out the way he/she plans. Always share a few household rules with them. Don't unload all of the rules at once. It might be too overwhelming for him/her to deal with. Remember, your heart is telling you that you want this to work out. If this is your first time giving this a chance, you won't be thinking negatively. Don't be naïve or overly cautious, because negative forces will become unavoidable. I share this information so that you will expect the unexpected and just know that you might not be living with the angel you hoped for. Hopefully, you did get a darling. But just in case you didn't, always be mindful that the children have a certain amount of street smarts. Some of them have a lot of street smarts. They can be master manipulators to get you to do what they want. They normally have a multitude of problems with their behavior. But, please remember this whenever possible, that you will stay the course and guide this child toward a better outcome in life. Some of them, you won't be able to get close enough to in order to help them. Most of them don't even act like children. They feel that they are grown already. That's one reason they are always listening to hear what they can capitalize on and what kind of information they can gather up as ammunition to use against you when they get ready to disrupt. If the child can't manipulate you and get things to work the way he/she wants them to work, he/she will start doing everything one can do to disrupt the placement. This is where your life seemingly begins to slowly go down hill. Remember, the child came to conquer and destroy the rules of your house. You can't afford to allow this to happen. Always maintain control of your household. But, you have to manage the child in a way that won't bring harm or damage to the child, your family or your property by de-escalation. Never try to bluff a child to calm him down; they will call your bluff. My advice to you at this point is: If you don't intend to act on a promise or threat to a child, never make it either. Find a way to communicate with this child by asking what is needed from you. If they have a problem you can help them with, you need to know what it is. This advice is Just-in-Case you end up in this type situation. To be totally honest with you, most of the times you won't get the type of child that you can develop a great relationship with but it won't be a child of horror, either. This is rare. Remember, when they're nice to you or do something for you, it is because they want something in return from you. Find out what it is that they want before you obligate yourself. They might want something that you can't deliver on and that will cause problems. They've lived their lives handling situations in this manner. When a child starts on the path of disruption, you have to be a very strong person to engage in the episodes of defiance. Notify the social worker, immediately. You need to know at what point you need to let go of this child because when a child is unhappy and doing all kinds of crazy stuff, you eventually get tired and worn down. You will be tempted to give up. Try to stay the course, but don't force really bad situations. Also, try time away from each other. I don't agree with the system that moves a child from home to home because of disruptions. My children and I have always discussed the fact that the first time a child creates a disruption, he/she needs to be sent off to a residential facility or boot camp to see how it is and promise them if they continue their unacceptable behavior, that's where they will be living and not in someone's home. That's just our opinion. But the system will move the child from home to home because that's what the child wants. This gives that child a free pass to continue the negative behavior of disrupting. Never feel down on yourself when you've done all you can do to help a child. I did that until I learned and saw that during the time the child was with me, I was able to bring a little stability and structure to the child's life even though a lot of them rebelled against it. The child doesn't realize that most good foster parents aren't going to just allow them to come in, conquer and destroy the rules of their home. Usually, when a child moves, he ends up in an even stricter environment than the one he/she was in before he/she set out to disrupt. Remember the time spent with you is of much consequence and value, because they begin to develop structure and gain some stability for that period of time. The longer the child stays with you, the more structure and stability he/she will have. Who knows, this might turn out to be a great child with your courage, determination, help and encouragement. I sincerely believe you can master this. Go ahead! Take a leap of faith! See what your state requirements are.

GET TO KNOW YOUR OPPONENT

You can't know the child you have in your home until he has settled in for about three weeks or more. If everything has gone well during this period, that's normal. We normally refer to this period as the "honeymoon period". After this time, you will probably begin to see unusual behaviors start coming alive. You will know that this isn't the same child that you met a few weeks ago.

This is the game plan. I'm telling you how to win. I wish I had someone to tell me. So, here is what you do. Purchase a journal, a very resourceful piece of equipment, and begin to write down all the information you find out about this child. At some point you will probably need this information to supply others or when incidents occur. You may need it to push someone's buttons before they can push yours sometimes. See, you are about to learn some things that will help you master these jobs. So, don't give up. You can be a great foster parent or substitute teacher. The children will never think so, but others will compliment you for doing a job well. The agency will praise you and you'll be the one they call for emergency respites. You might enjoy respite pay. They love it when a foster parent knows how to use their training. They especially love it when you can handle yourself with the children and not have to call them all the time for every little thing. For instance, when I start getting to know a child

21

in my home, I begin to ask questions. I secretly record the information for later use. It's invaluable. You need to find out what the child likes or loves, what kind of entertainment he/she likes, the places he/she likes to go, who the friends are and their addresses and phone numbers. Your caller I.D is a great tool to use to acquire numbers associated with the child. You need to know addresses and names of relatives that live nearby. If you are as good as I am at investigating, then you are able to tell the agency some things they don't even know. It happens with me all the time. You should be a great listener for any and all information. You should know about how much the child weighs and be able to give a good description of the child, just in case he/she decides to runaway. Find some reason to get a personal photograph of the child in case he/she runs away or is missing. You can't be a good investigator if you don't jot down all the clues. Let me tell you about one situation. I had a 16-year-old white female, who was in love with a 21-year-old black male, come to live with me once. It doesn't matter how you preach against relationships like this at this age, you will always meet with resistance. Her family was also in resistance and I could truly understand their concerns. This was a beautiful girl, age 16, hanging out with a dude not attending school, wasn't working anywhere and he was 21 years old. He was staying with some of his friends. The girl and I talked with each other a lot. I don't feel we were close because I couldn't trust her. I think she liked me, but she loved her boyfriend. We went through several incidents together. Let me show you how getting information helped. The social worker and agency I worked for had forbidden this boy to ever be in contact with this child. He was 21 years old and that was enough reason for her not to be seeing him. On one occasion, my youngest daughter had taken the girl shopping at a little mall near where I live. On their way home, the girl saw her boyfriend and briefly stopped to talk to him. I've trained my children to let me know what goes on when the foster children are out with them. So, my daughter remembered the location and how to get back to it. She told me about the foster child talking to a boy in some apartments near the mall. I wrote that piece of information down. When my foster child went with her parents on a respite, to give us a break from each other, I had my daughter drive me to the mall and we got the address of the apartment complex where the boyfriend was living. I didn't even think that I would need the information. I just thought it was best to have it if something ever came up. Sure enough, a few weeks passed and the boy had made his way to my house at 11:30 PM, at night! I heard the girl talking to someone from her bedroom, which was located on the front side of the house. By the way, I've learned that it's best not to have a telephone or television in the child's room because that gives them too much access to negative forces. You will create problems for yourself if you supply them with these items. Now, back to my story. When I heard his voice, I opened my front door and invited him off my property. I threatened to call the police if he didn't leave. He left and I thought things would go back to normal. She was in her room, with the radio on and her door locked. So, I thought. The Spirit told me to check outside the house. I ignored the inner voice and passed by her room, noticing she hadn't come out since he left. I was prompted to go out to check again. I didn't dismiss the prompting that time. When I got around the side of the house, the window was up. She had crawled out the window, left the screen on the bed, the light and radio was on, with her door locked from the inside. I put the screen back in place, went back into the house, let the window down and locked it. To do this, I had to break into her room, by slamming my body's weight into the door, pushing it open. I cut the light out. I called the on-call person at my agency to notify them. I was told to wait a little while before calling the police to get an incident report. About 12:30 AM I called the police. I gave them her description and all the information I had, including telephone numbers and addresses so they could write a report. The next morning, a lady officer called to see if I wanted them to storm the apartment complex where I thought she was and I told them to go get her. She ended up spending nearly a day in jail because I wouldn't go get her. I told her when she called me that I wouldn't go to jail for my own kids for doing what she did and that I wouldn't be coming to get her. I told her I would notify her social worker. Her social worker would have to get her out. She hated being behind bars with the criminals. She said she was so afraid. She later told me when she came by my house about 4:30 AM, she saw the light out and knew I had discovered what she had done. She kept going. She told me she saw a police car and hid in some bushes where a flight of bats flew into her. She was terrified. She hitched a ride with some young men from the high school that she knew and had them take her to where her boyfriend was living with his friends near the mall. The second time she ran away, the agency put her out of their program. She was almost about to age out of the system anyway. The young lady called me a few years later to tell me that everything I tried to tell her was right. She said she had to cut that boyfriend lose. She hooked up with another boy and got pregnant. She said her baby girl was two years old and she was working as a cashier at a grocery store. I feel she started living too early and she wasn't married. She was the kind of young lady that a young man could easily convince to go astray. This is sad, but she sounded like she was being responsible to do what was necessary to sustain her life for her and her baby. After that conversation, I tried calling her and discovered she had changed her number to an unlisted one. I don't know what brought that about. In this experience, I begin to learn how to deal with foster children. You have to know how far you can go and sometimes you have to allow them to make bad choices and pay the consequences. Don't be critical and don't judge them because they think they know everything. They are slightly different from your children and you can't take them to the woodshed like you can your own.

I can't stress to you enough, the need not to reveal the information about yourself or what may be going on in your life to them. When you're upset, they are listening for the reason you are upset and before long after they find out, they will use that same information to upset you. I am amazed at all the ways and things these children have picked up in their lifetime. They have a very keen sense of hearing.

They will literally get down on the floor to hear what you're talking about. They will go into a room adjacent to where you are just to hear what is going on. They listen to hear if you're walking to find out if you are going somewhere so they can ask if they can go. But they mostly listen for ways to get in your head to push your buttons. They want to know the details of your business.

CARE, CHOICES, CONSEQUENCES AND CONSISTENCY

care enough to make sure the child knows what is expected of him/her. I make sure they are listening by modeling good listening skills. I ask them if they understand what I'm saying to them. I don't always raise my voice when I'm upset with them, now that I've learned better. It throws them off when you handle situations calmly. I try to speak softly and not judge or criticize them. I explain to the child that I care and I am concerned about the choices he/she makes. I constantly and always remind all my children to make the right choices. I may reward them in some circumstances, but I don't want them to think that it's only right to make right choices when you are going to get a reward. Bribery is just not good for children. They don't learn the appropriate lesson from it. I explain to them that making the right choices is just the right thing to do. You don't want them being good to get paid for it or just to be rewarded. You have to make them understand that they must do right because they are supposed to do what's good and right.

I always explain or remind my children of the results of making the wrong choices. We teach them and train them right or wrong, we model the right thing to do in front of them and we let them know that we expect them to handle situations the right way, so they will end up with the right outcome. Some children will make the wrong choices because of what they feel is peer pressure and what someone else will think or feel about his/her decision. This is totally unacceptable. It's inexcusable for a child to know the right choice to make and then decide not to.

After the child has been trained in making the right choices and there is clear evident that he/she is doing wrong, it becomes necessary to teach them about the consequences of their actions and what the actions could cost them. You explain to them that their unacceptable behavior will cause a privilege to be taken away. It could be restricted playtime, no television or game playing. This is also a good time to begin to instill in them, the fact that if they act up at school or anywhere else, they will be dealt with at home through consequences. They need to learn that misbehaving is unacceptable anywhere.

If you are not an enforcer of consequences, it will lead to inconsistencies and a child will pick up on the fact that nothing will be done to him/her. This will eventually lead to repetitive behavior problems. You aren't doing yourself or anyone else any favors by not exacting consequences and not being consistent. Some children have a multitude of problems that would lead to consequences all their life. I have had children who were always doing something unacceptable. I had to come to the realization that you can't send them to the room for everything. You'll end up driving yourself over the edge. So, you learn how to pick your battles. The behaviors that would most likely lead to destruction or harmful damage to their lives are the ones I would pick to deal with. I call it picking my battles. I keep a calendar for my child and me to keep up with his/her time in the "Think-Tank". This is what we call the child's room. Assigning the child days to his/her room is one of the only consequences that will work sometimes. He/she has no privileges when in the room. When you find assigning one or two days in there doesn't work, you need to increase it by a week and keep increasing it until it get's their attention. Sometimes, I've had to get a chair and sit in the hall by the child's room to make sure he didn't come out. I believe in serious consequences. If the child is doing something like making excuses to come out to go to the bathroom every ten minutes, after that second visit, I tell them it's going to cost you a day of consequences every time you ask to go. They hate the additional days. So if they don't want to pay with a day, they'll stop repeatedly asking to go. Make sense to me. For whatever mischief he/she does while in the room, charge an additional day or be creative and come up with some other consequence. I had a child that would tear up paper and put it all over the room, just have the room in such disarray. To solve this problem, I walked up to the door, reached for the handle and said to him, when you get this room cleaned up the way it should be, I'll open this door. I don't like seeing the way you are treating my Kingdom, so this door must remain closed until we have order in here again. I'll ask him if he understands and then close the door. This is why it is so important for you to get to know your child. He knows you and how to push your buttons. He knows what you don't like and how to irritate you when he is trying to manipulate you. You need to know his/her likes and dislikes and use them to correct him/her. These children normally want to rule your world. I knew this child wanted to know every movement in the house and wanted to hear everything that was said. He would never want his door closed. I know he hates being in the room when he has to be in there. He told his therapist he hates being in there. You've got to take advantage of the knowledge you acquire. Make it work for you. Anytime I walk by his room and he has scattered things all everywhere, I reach and get the doorknob and close the door. A few minutes later, I'll hear him hollering, "It's cleaned up", and I'll go open the door. I think supposedly normal children have the same tendencies, but maybe less frequent. You've had time to work with your own children and mold them into the way they should grow. Whatever they have to do to get attention, negative or positive, some foster children will do it. They will try to wear you down to make their world the way they want it. They watch to see if you're going to feel sorry for them and let them out of their consequences early and if you do, they feel as if they have won something. They have. You must always be consistent when you give consequences. The child will most likely be angry with you, but at least you will establish a pattern of consistency with him/her. I tell them if they do the crime, they must do the time. Give consequences when they refuse to do things that you've asked them to do. They will refuse to do what you say, then spend time crying and having a tantrum, and then tell you they're hungry. All this is to avoid doing what you've asked them to do and still get what they want. Tell them that you haven't eaten either and when he/she does what you told them to do, you both can eat together. Tell him/her that you are prepared to stay up with them all night to make sure they do what they are asked. Play this out and mean what you say to them and soon, when the hunger pains begin to really hit them and they see you mean every word you speak to them; they'll start doing what you ask. Don't you give in to them, but hold out until they do what you want them to. You will be building strength for yourself, gaining knowledge for future conflicts and taking control of the situation. Afterwards, you might even feel like grinning at the situation. Just don't allow them to see you laughing. Have a 'you're not going to win this one buddy' look on your face. Sometimes these situations will take several hours to resolve, so you must allow time to be on your side. It's worth the time spent if it gets you your desired result. I can't guarantee this will work for every child or every situation. But, it does work. That's why I stress getting to know his/her likes and dislikes so you can armor up.

Sometimes the child will holler and scream to the top of his/her voice. They know you won't like this and think you don't have a solution. Always keep you a headphone or earphone to be used with a CD player, radio or cassette player. When they go off into that loud tantrum mode, take your equipment and go in their room with them, shut the door and get hooked up to your source of music, turn it up loud, close your eyes and begin to sing out loud. I will get up and practice a Praise dance at times. They'll think you're crazy. But you'll like the results. If they say something to you, you won't hear them because your music will be drowning them out. I get a kick out of doing this. I believe by the time we finish these tips on fostering, you will feel as if you can master it, too. I believe you can. We need good foster parents who are willing to stay the course as long as they can. In order to do this, you have to know that you have spiritual help to assist you along the way. The Holy Spirit will guide you in all your ways if you invite Him in. He's your ace in the hole. You will understand why I call it a great job. It allows you to be your own boss. It helps you create a more stable individual to send out into society. You will feel you've done your best to help a child be the best he/she can be. That's very rewarding. The child is usually gone to school or involved in extracurricular activities. During these times, you can enjoy much peace. You should rest up and do nice things for yourself. You'll be ready to go another round with him/her when he/she returns. It's time to start dealing with the behaviors again. The child's idea is to wear you down and cause you not to want to foster him/her. But they can't because you're getting the necessary breaks away from them to keep you energized. They get to a point in time when they can't disrupt at home then school is the next target on the list. I always tell mine, if you get in trouble at school, then you're in trouble at home and will be given the same consequences. If you are consistent, they'll believe and will at least try to work on their behavior. If they don't believe and continue to get in trouble, you should carry out the consequences. The consequence may not always succeed, but more and longer the consistency, the more changes you will probably see. Always remind them that they are the children and you are the adult. You can't let them forget this.

THE NEED TO MANIPULATE
AND CONTROL

All children have the instinct to manipulate you if they think they can get what they want. Unfortunately, manipulation is a way of life that seems to be ingrained in the minds of most foster children. There are so many ways that a child will try to make things happen in his/her life. Do a study on the word manipulation. Google it up if you have that capability. Go to the library and look it up. It's an ugly behavior that I find hard to tolerate. I don't like it when a child tries to get in my head just to get something he/she wants, but they do and they will. Our job is to try to break the bad habit. It won't be easy because it is a way of life for them. I tell them they'd stand a better chance of getting something from me by just asking me for it. But that won't stop them from trying. They've lived their lives learning and having success with this method. Manipulation is unacceptable to me in any form. I've had a child who has actually been brought to tears because he couldn't manipulate my son or me. When manipulation didn't work for him, he started shedding tears. I asked what was wrong and the answer he gave me didn't make any sense. He started giving me a scenario that came totally from out of left field and didn't even apply to what was actually going on. He didn't know that I knew why he was crying. I kept pressing him for an answer until he finally admitted that it was because he couldn't get us to do what he wanted. At that point, I assured him that he would never be able to manipulate or control us. When your child volunteers to do something nice, usually the child has expectations of you doing something for him in return. When he doesn't get what he/she was working for, he/she ends up upset and angry. If you haven't dealt with manipulation before, you probably won't even know why he/she is upset. I've learned that this is something they've learned along the way and probably the only way they feel they can get what they feel they need or want. I'm sure it's very disappointing when things don't work out for them. I ask them why they don't just ask for what they want. I tell them my answer will be yes, no, or maybe and 'no' won't kill you. If I thought 'no' would kill you, well then we might be able to work something else out.

Now let's get to the issue of control. At the first episode, after a child comes to live in my home, I tell them that my home is my Kingdom and I am Queen. God is my King, but He Allows me to rule and reign. I never allow children to rule and reign in my Kingdom. I tell them I own everything in my Kingdom. For them to look at or play with anything in my Kingdom is a privilege. I say to them 'if you, disrespect me, disobey me or is destructive with anything that is mine, you'll lose your privilege to touch it.' I tell them if they continue to do what I tell them not to do with my things in my Kingdom, they'll lose the privilege to handle my stuff. I have to show them I mean what I say. I tell them sometimes you can lose privileges and never be able to earn them back. I have six grandkids and a foster child. My grandkids come and spend every other weekend with me and usually they are with me the entire summer. I've trained them to try to work things out among themselves before bringing the problem to me. My grandkids can spend an entire weekend with me and I never have a problem with them sharing or working things out. But time my foster child is in the mix, the problems arrive. I have a satellite dish that's programmable with a remote control. I told my foster child never to program my television to record 30-minute pro-grams. I reserve that feature for movies in case I lose the signal on the satellite and I still have power. He ignored me and just did it anyway. I took the remote from him for about 3 weeks. Then, I thought I'd give him another chance. I wasn't gone out of the room for 10 min-utes after handing him my remote before he started programming 30-minute programs into the machine. In addition to being disobe-dient to what I had said, he lied and said he didn't do it. He was the only child present in the house at the time and the only one who could have done it. He was nine years old, smart as a whip, made the A/B honor roll at school and just as defiant as he wanted to be. So, I stopped allowing him to touch my remote. Usually, he's in trouble and has to stay in the Think-Tank when the grandkids come to visit. But, if he isn't in trouble, he's allowed to be part of the crew. He always creates drama when he's in the mix. In order to be fair in the Kingdom, I end up taking the remote control and programming the television for each one of them. Everybody gets a 30-minute choice. I program it for all day whether they're watching the program or not. Even when he's the only one home, I program the television for him when he's not in trouble because of his disobedience. I know he loves to watch television, so I get to push his buttons. I guess you think by now that I'm a control freak. I have to admit that I am when it comes to these children. I love it! When he disrespects me, as he sometimes does, I decide I don't want to watch television in my room. I want to watch the bigger screen. So, guess what? I have to keep my remote in my room, because he is the type of child that does underhanded stuff behind your back and lie about it. So, I go to the television where he is and put it on a station I know he doesn't like to watch and I'll sit for a couple of hours and watch what I want. Right now, I'm doing the button pushing. Sometimes he'll say "I don't like whatever is on" and I'll say well you don't respect me either, so I don't really care about what you like. I tell him, I can't get you to do what I like. So, I'm not going to do what you like. I think that's fair. He's one to think you forget about the unacceptable things he does. He'll try to talk real friendly and be nice and accommodating the next day (trying to get the outcome that he wants: (MANIPULATION!). I talk real nice and friendly to him and I proceed to take my remote and put it on something I know he doesn't like to watch. You see God didn't leave you helpless or hopeless. He invented controls for the television just for you and me. The remote is there just so we would have a way to teach the darlings about respect. If it's in your house, it belongs to you. Use it! I might do this for a week or even two at a time. It has caused him to consider his loss if he is disrespectful toward me for the moment. He's impulsive. He'll do it again and again and again and so will I. So, until the next time, it's another something I can laugh about silently. When he comes home in the evening and I'm there watching what I want to watch on television, it ruins his whole evening. He hates watching the news. I get a kick out of his attitude. He'll sit down on the sofa and when he gets tired of watching what I'm watching, he'll make a statement about some show he likes to watch. I ignore him because I really don't care about that at the time. I'm thinking how disrespectful you were to me. I've learned that you can't just read one book and know how to deal with foster children or any child. You have to be determined, get advice and be creative. You have to show these children that if they can be disrespectful to you in your Kingdom, then you don't have to satisfy their whims. I tell them my responsibility is to provide you a roof over your head, food to eat, guidance and a safe environment. Anything else is a privilege. I tell him I go out of my way trying to get along with him, but sometimes I'm not going to concern myself with his behavior. I'll just model his behavior to him to allow him to see or feel what it's like to be disrespected and ignored. I tell him that's how I feel when you treat me that way and every time you disrespect or ignore what I'm telling you, I'm going to model your behavior back to you. I'm in control of my Kingdom and I make a conscious decision that if I'm not happy, my problem child isn't going to be happy either. I do the same thing when my grandkids come over and simply mess up my house. I get my remote control, put the television on pause or shut it off sometimes, until they clean my house up. I tell them when I am here alone, my house is clean and I refuse to allow you to come over and have my house in such disarray. I don't even have to tell my grandkids to clean it up. The moment I pause my television, the team immediately gets up and get to work. I tell them that I don't have to have them over to my house and if they're not going to help keep it clean, I'd rather they stay home.

My foster child is very destructive with his toys and anybody else's. Yet, he is always asking if he can play with my PlayStation or play on my computer. He won't listen when I tell him to take care of his things better. I tell him when I see that you've learn to take care of your things. I might allow you to play with mine when I have time to supervise. I let him know that I'm not going to allow him to tear up my stuff. I tell him my grandkids need something to play with when they visit. You should allow no one to rule and reign over your Kingdom unless it's your King.

The children have been through some tough times if they're in the system. We can make things more difficult for them or we can have teachable moments with them. Make sure the child's social worker know everything that's going on with the child. If you think there may be a situation that could put a family member in jeopardy, talk to the social worker and make the best decision for your family. There is so much you don't know about the children when you bring them into your home. Get all the information you can from whatever source is available. You need to know if they lie, steal and do other things you wouldn't agree with. You don't want to be lied on or have one of your family members lied on. The children have a Bill of Rights and I'm sure in most places, the family has rights also. I have said before that I write down information. I make incident and behavior reports on the children These reports help me function better in what I'm trying to accomplish. Sometimes I know the child better than his parents or social worker. That's because I am with them more and I want to know everything about them I can because they are living in my home. When I get information, I want to know how I can use it to help the child. What can I do to get this child to trust me? Even though the children have behavior problems, there's an unknown reason that causes the child to do what he/she does. I have been fortunate at times to figure out what is going on in their heads. Most of the time, they don't know themselves why they act the way they do. It's hard to get information from these children. If they ever begin to trust you, don't violate their trust. If you learn something that might be harmful to them or someone else and they won't talk to you, try to see if they will talk to their social worker or counselor, or some other person they might be close to. If you can help them with the problem, then by all means help them. Let them know that you have to encourage them to share the information with their social worker or therapist and you can't just sit on the information if someone is in danger. But tell them you will go with them and be there for them. The plan is not to cause setbacks, but to move these children forward to better circumstances. A lot of the children have lost faith and hope and you can't live a joyous life without either of these attributes. So, it's good to know how to deal with situations of manipulation, control and defiance. There's lots of good advice on the Internet. You should research the issue of fostering. Remember, you are not alone in your decision. Sometimes you might think you made a mistake, but you can never make a mistake trying to guide a child in the way he/she should go. We, too, once were children.

Don't forget to praise the children for the good things they do and the accomplishments they make. Praise is a force that will cause them to press forward and strive to do better. Everyone would like a shout-out every now and then and these children are no different from the rest of us in that respect. Even praise them for the efforts they make to try to accomplish things. Show appreciation and encouragement for even the smallest things they attempt to do better. They want to know that you are noticing them. They crave that attention. They feel like somebody cares enough to notice.

SUPPORT GROUPS

A parent support group offers a safe environment for traditional parents and foster/adoptive parents. Parents meet to foster better communication and exchange ideas or knowledge. A support group offers a non-judgmental environment where people can express their views and problems and also, learn how others are providing solutions to problems. These meetings provide educational opportunities for all the members, while growing individually and as a group, all in the spirit of fun. You need a support system when you are doing foster care. Someone you can share your specific problems with as they relate to the child you're fostering or your own biological children. With everyone talking about their individual problems and others having been through some of the identical situations, the meetings makes for a great bonding tool. Even when there is not a meeting going on, you can call each other up and discuss what's going on and be a sounding board for one another. The information you obtain gives you great solutions to some difficult problems. You learn about other resources where you can go for help, that you wouldn't ordinarily know about, if you didn't attend some of the meetings or have a bond with one of the other parents with whom you share information.

Another tool that will help provide relief for you is respite. A respite is where another parent will provide care for your child while you get a much needed break, because those times will surely come. A respite is always good for both parties in the sense that being away from each other will bring about refreshment and a new perspective for the adult and the child. In most cases I know, one respite a month is provided for you at no cost. This may be different in places other than Alabama. You would need to check with your recruiter person for the answer. Always question the social worker about family visits. This would add to your list of resources if visitations are allowed. The problem with some family visits is that some family members will stir up strife. They might give the child erroneous information to cause problems in your home and which will make it difficult for you to foster the child. Normally after a family visit, a child will come to your home acting worst than he did before he left for any number of reasons. You have to be aware that even through telephone conversations, family members can cause problems. The best way to deal with problems of this nature is through the child's social worker. The social worker can arrange supervised visits or if it is thought that the family is the cause of your problems and they continue to stir up strife, the visits and phone calls can be discontinued until the family agrees to stop causing problems for the child.

Activities and outings are other ways to provide rest relief for you, like weeklong camps, summer camps and church activities. There are many organizations that sponsor activities for foster children. Sometimes your own family members outside your household can help you with your children. You are not without help or support or rest breaks. The focus is to stay powered-up. The idea is to outlast your opponent. You can't do that if you don't take care of yourself.

THE MATTER OF FINANCES

You're probably wondering what finances have to do with fostering a child. I'm writing about finances because of the type of experiences I've had in this area. A lot of children come to you feeling like the world owes them a debt. Some of them know you are being reimbursed for their care and they think you're supposed to spend all that money on them. They will constantly worry you about things they want. They will nag you to get whatever they want. You have to explain to them that you are being reimbursed so that you can provide a safe environment for him/her, help pay the increased utility bills brought on with his/her presence, help provide gas for taking him/her on medical appointments, picking him/her up from school or other activities, help buy shoes, clothes and give him/her an allowance. They won't be convinced of that, but at least you would have taken the time to try to explain things to them. They don't understand or care about budgeting or anything like that. I had a child that didn't like for me to confront him about anything like obeying rules. So, when I would confront him about wrongdoing, he would exact revenge by running the household water for long periods of time. He would tear off more than necessary amount of tissue he needed until you would have to replace it. That's why I keep saying, "don't talk and allow them to hear what you're upset about", because they'll do it to push your button. It satisfies them to do something you don't like and they will use it over and over again. They feel that's the only way to strike back at you and maybe you'll get so tired of them pushing your buttons until you'll just call the social worker up and say come and get him out of my house. I have been very creative to curb some of these issues. When they finish using up the rolls of tissue, I simply tell them that I had plans to take them shopping and let them buy themselves something. Then, I tell them I can't do it now because I am going to spend the money on toilet tissue or the water bill. Most of the time that would really be my intention. So, it cost them a trip shopping and the opportunity to buy something for themselves. I usually get a remark like "Ah, man!" I explain that all these things like wasting up toilet tissue and running the water unnecessarily cost me money and that it is more important to have tissue paper and running water in the house, than going shopping. Then, I ask if they understand and tell them they will see how it is when they grow up and have to spend their money on their children.

Other ways they will get you is playing over food or telling you they don't like or eat certain foods. Every time the child tells you he doesn't like a certain food, write it in your journal. Sometimes, if you know he likes a certain food, you'll prepare it for him. He wants to push your buttons when he tell you he don't eat that. He wont remember that you served it to him a couple of weeks ago and he didn't have a problem eating it. Remember he said he didn't eat this certain dish, then wait until he's feeling all right and is in a good mood, prepare that dish but give him something else. Remind him of what he said a couple of weeks ago. Prepare him something else instead. I am giving you so much ammunition, there's no way you can fail at this.

ROAD MAP TO SUCCESS

I am always thinking of ways to make life easier for me in fostering children. I think every foster parent should have some rules written down and posted somewhere the child can be constantly reminded of what is expected of him/her. Don't give them any excuse to disobey. You need to go over the rules with them often. I am including a sample of my rules in this writing.

GUIDELINES FOR THIS HOME

The Den Area

Always leave the den area neat. If you drop paper on the floor, pick it up and put it in the trash. Do not leave notebooks, papers, pencils or school materials in the den. They should be kept in your room. If you find this area clean, when you leave it to go your room, it should be left clean. Do not bring food or beverages to this area. Please eat at the bar or the kitchen table.

The Kitchen Area

Please wash your hands in the bathroom or at the kitchen sink before handling dishes, food or going into the refrigerator. It's just the sanitary thing to do. When you finish eating, please properly put leftover food on your plate in the trash. If you only have 3 items to be washed, (i.e., a plate, glass and fork) please rinse these items and place them near the sink to be washed when there are more dishes. If there are dishes there already, place the stopper in the sink and make the dish-water by adding several drops of dishwashing liquid to hot running water, making sure the water is not too hot for your hands. Then, proceed to wash the dishes. Pots and pans are dishes, too. If they are on the stove, please don't leave them for someone else to wash. Never use your hands and dishwashing liquid to wash the dishes. That isn't sanitary. If you have questions about anything, feel free to ask them.

The Bedroom Area

Keeping your bedroom clean is your responsibility, even if you allow your visiting family member or a friend to share your room. You should allow yourself time to leave it clean before you go to school or on a trip. Candy wrapper papers shouldn't be left on the floor. Trash should be taken to the trash container near the kitchen. Clean clothes should be ironed and hung up on hangers or put in drawers. Dirty clothes should be put in a basket in your closet waiting to be laundered.

The Bathroom Area

You will be responsible for keeping the bathroom that you use clean. I will provide the necessary cleaning products to use for cleaning. I will be happy to show you how to clean. There are times when you will need to sweep or mop the bathroom as part of your chores. Please make sure it is cleaned, as often as needed because when company comes, that is the bathroom that they will use. The paper towels in the bathroom are primarily for visitors to dry their hands. Please don't use them up. You have access to towels and face cloths. Please keep the wastebasket in the bathroom emptied into the trash container located near the kitchen area.

My Bedroom

My bedroom is totally of limits unless you're invited. Children are not allowed without my permission. If you need to visit the Internet for an assignment. I will be present or I will provide you with the research you need.

YOUR PERSONAL RESPONSIBILITIES

Respect Persons In Authority: Home (foster parent, family members)
School (principal, teacher, adults)
Church (pastor, adult leaders, parents)
Community (police, adult leaders, parents)

Permission: Ask permission to go places and to participate in any activity that involves my participation. Please do not assume that it is all right to do anything you want. Please do not make personal plans before discussing them with me.

Decisions: Please be able to accept "NO" responses to requests.

Phone Time: Please do not continuously tie up the phone line with your personal calls. The telephone is a privilege that can be lost if abused. Don't even get on the phone if you haven't done chores or homework. You will lose the privilege.

How to Handle Your Problems: If you have a problem living in this home, please come and discuss it with me to see if we can resolve it. If we can't, then we will discuss it with the agency and DHR. If you have a problem with the children at school, don't let it get out of hand before you tell someone in authority. You can tell the principal or the assistant principal. You can also tell the counselor. Do not take matters into your own hands.

Grades: It is your responsibility to study and make passing grades. It is also your responsibility to seek help before you find yourself failing in a subject. Failing grades/unacceptable behavior will bring a loss of privileges. Passing grades/acceptable behavior will earn you rewards and privileges.

Sign: _____ Sign: _____
Date:_____

WINNING WAYS

1. Have a pleasant attitude.
2. Say, Good morning or Hell-o in the afternoon. It costs nothing to speak.
3. Be considerate.
4. Don't be an all about me person.
5. Watch your tone of voice with people.
6. Show yourself friendly and willing to help without being asked.
7. Don't do shoddy work. Do a good job to show you are capable.
8. Never do just enough to get what you want.
9. Do things out of the goodness of your heart if there is goodness in there.
10. Don't expect people to dance to your music. You don't dance to theirs.
11. Give and it shall be given to you. Do things for others and they will do things for you.
12. The world doesn't owe you anything; so stop acting like it does.

13. If you always expect people to do things for you, what have you done for them lately?
14. If you hang around the wrong group of people, you will become just like them. If they get in trouble, you will end up in trouble, also.
15. If you make good choices, you will get good consequences, but if you make bad choices, you will receive bad consequences.

After the child has been in my home for a few days, I take a portion of the guidelines and go over it with them. I might have to modify the document depending upon the age of the child to make it age appropriate. When we finish the entire document, I ask the child if there is anything he/she doesn't understand/ if they have questions, I answer them. I allow the child to sign the document and then I sign and date it. Then I run the child off a copy to keep in his/her room. It serves notice that we have gone over the rules of the house and we understand them. When there is an occurrence of an incident relative to one of the situations listed in the guidelines, the child can't say that I hadn't been over it with him/her or he/she didn't know. Now, don't think because you have this document, problems won't arise. They will. The signed guidelines are especially good if you have a lying child living with you. When you read the guidelines, you will discover many problems you are bound to encounter as a foster parent. I just don't want you to be blind-sided by any of them. Just like any job, you'll have good days and bad days. But the information I have provided you, gives you the chance to turn your bad days into good days.

Please note the list of behaviors or conditions that you will most likely have to deal with if you are specifically doing therapeutic foster care:

Manipulation
Anger
Anxiety
Impulsiveness

Low self-image
Oppositional defiance
Retaliation
Mood swings
Inability to connect feelings with behavior
Expects rewards that are not consistent with his/her behavior
Irrational statements
Food is a comforter
Disrespect Adult Authority
Likes to be center of attention
Lies
Wants control

I have dealt with all of the listed behaviors in one child. This was a challenging case. You don't have the behaviors showing up all at once or at the same time; therefore you can choose the worst to deal with. But always be consistent when you are dealing with the issues. Knowledge is power and you will gain power if you read up on some of the information provided. I am telling you that all the things I have written about, I have experienced with children. I survived and you will too. It sounds worst than it actually is. The need for good foster parents is so great. The number of children being drawn into the system is seriously increasing everyday. The economy is wreaking havoc on families today, especially low-income families. God has a great big heart and he expects us to have big hearts, too. Will you open your heart for one of God's children who need someone like you? Will you allow Him to come in and work with you to help a child reach a better outcome? It's not an easy job, but it can be very rewarding. I have had so many people to tell me that they don't see how I do foster care. This is how I feel about it. I raised three children to become adults and I have six living grandchildren. If something were to happen to my family that prevented us from being able to take care of our children, I would want a loving foster parent to be there for them. I read an article in the newspaper and was in awe at the story and Virginia Holloway, the young lady that wrote it. I e-mailed her to get permission to include the story in my book. She said yes and here it is:

Foster Care Opens Future For Kids
By: Virginia Holloway

She was born on a cold, snowy day in February 1978. She was welcomed home by her big sister and brother, mother and father.

Soon things began to change. Family members and neighbors could see that as the baby's dad went to work, she would need more assistance than her mom could offer. The family helped; her brother went to live with his grandmother, and her sister to live with her grandmother.

Five years passed, and it was time for the little girl to start school. Sometimes, it would be raining or cold, and she would get to school late. Oftentimes, she would walk with her mom. Sometimes, she would not have clean clothes, and she was not clean. The little girl would curse at the teachers and principal. The school became concerned. The little girl had a great caring and loving teacher, Mrs. Little.

The school tried to help, but could not. So someone who was concerned called the Department of Human Resources, more commonly known as DHR. DHR sent out one of its people, a social worker. Her name was Mrs. White. She found someone, an aunt, for the little girl to stay with. The aunt did not know how long the little girl would be with her.

The little girl went to school, and her classmates did not know her because there was such a change. She had on new clothes.

The little girl was behind in school. She did not know many common things like her alphabet, numbers or colors when she started school. But her aunt began to work steadily with her. The little girl remembers having to sit at the table every night and practice. Eventually, the little girl caught up to her classmates. She began making the honor roll, and her behavior improved.

The little girl enjoyed being with her aunt, but she also enjoyed spending time on the weekends and holidays with her family. She enjoyed riding bikes with her brother and talking on the phone with her sister.

The little girl grew into a young woman. She continued doing well in school. A social worker continued to see her every month, just to check on her. There were several community members who helped motivate the young woman. They assisted her in competing in area competitions such as Junior Miss, and also helped her in going to Washington D.C., and representing Bibb County.

The young woman realized this social worker made a difference in her life. So the young woman decided to become a social worker.

She graduated from high school with honors and started college. She earned her bachelor's degree in social work. She then started to work with children who had come from the same place she had. She hope to change the lives of those children by finding them foster and adoptive homes, with loving parents to help them learn and reach their potential.

Would you consider opening your heart and sharing your home with a foster child? You might just raise the next social worker, firefighter, doctor, member of Congress, or judge. Give a child a chance.

I am the little girl in this story, and I am proud to say a social worker and a dedicated foster home changed my life and helped make me a success. I would like to say thank you to my Aunt Judy, Mr. Herbie, Mrs. Covington, Granny Parker and all my social workers: Mrs. White, Mrs. Carol and Mrs. Judy.

This article was published in The Birmingham News, February 7, 2010 and was written by Social Worker, Virginia Holloway. Ms. Holloway earned her Bachelor's of Social Work (BSW) at the University of Alabama at Birmingham and her Master's of Social Work (MSW) at the University of Alabama at Tuscaloosa.

I appreciate Ms. Holloway's willingness to share this article and I hope it moves you to make a wonderful difference in the life of a child. I hope the blueprint I have shared with you is enough information to erase any fears you might have and challenge you and others to meet the needs of children everywhere. You won't be alone. There's always someone to help and encourage you. You can do this! Start your journey soon!

SUBSTITUTE TEACHER: ANOTHER LOVELY WORLD

Before I introduce you to this other world, I must address some of today's issues. The economy is in crisis. The 'there are no jobs' statement is not all true. There are jobs all around you. It may not be the type of job you are use to or desire, but there are jobs. You know what, God need people to fill these jobs, God would expect you to create a job. President Obama is busy trying to deal with grid-lock in Washington and world affairs. While he is trying to stay afloat dealing with people who want him to fail, why would people be looking to him to create jobs when they should be looking to God. God is the source and President Obama is His instrument. People are missing the mark here. God put in my spirit the thought that there are jobs everywhere. Because of all the hatred being stirred up, I was concerned about the President and his family, but I rest assured that God will take care of them. A word to those who think they are wise should be sufficient. Anybody that God allows to be President (Democrat or Republican) is God's family. He created family, so when you try to destroy the individual, you're messing with God's family. The older generation used to say 'if you dig one ditch, you

50

better dig two, cause the one you're digging will be for you. I'd like to add a little rhyme to that statement. It just might be your waterloo! So, the election process is over and I want to do my best to help the party in power. When I think of my children and grandchildren, I feel it's my duty to focus on ways to help them and others succeed in their lives. I can't seem to grasp the fact that people who are used to making more money than minorities don't want minorities to survive. If you make three times the salary that others make, how can you not see a disparity there? How can minorities have good family structures if mom and dad have to work three or four jobs just to make ends meet? How do you raise good kids if you're never home with them to attend to their needs? If parents aren't financially able to take care of their families because they can't bring in enough income, it may cause them to have to give their children up. There are serious inequities in our country still, people. I thank God that all rich people aren't fighting against the poor in this country. Our eyes are opened and there are those rich people who couldn't care less about the poor in America. I am one who was denied promotions on jobs that I worked because of my race and my stand against injustice. We, in poverty, look at others in this country taking their families to the beach or to the Bahamas and we can't even afford to go to the grocery store to feed our families. God is Love and those who don't love are not of Him. There are people afraid that they're going to lose their riches and they will lose it because of fear. They know the reasons they are afraid. How can we be ONE nation of people when the rich hates the poor and can only show a lack of concern for them? I must get back on task. Time demands for people who have gotten up in age and need relief now to be helped. They don't have time to go back to school to be educated for a new career. They need something now! Foster parenting and substitute teaching may not be the jobs of choice, but the positions will bring needed income to the family and these positions only require several hours of training. Others should be coming up with ideas and ways to make conditions better for everyone in America and not just better for a mere few. It's time for all to begin to use the gift of their minds to create jobs. Most of us want to do the job that we want to do. We've spoiled ourselves. We need to do the jobs that need to be done in order to raise or maintain our standards of living. I grew up wanting to be a teacher. My experience as a substitute teacher has helped me to realize that I wouldn't want to have a career as a teacher today. When I grew up you didn't have the behavior problems you have today. I believe the behaviors come from parents having to work jobs that are taking them away from the home and the children. So, now I say thank God, who knew what it would be like when I became old enough to become a teacher. I was steered in another direction. I always try to tackle the things I don't want to do. Well, most of the time. I've always wanted to help children learn. So, I plan to start an academic enrichment program through my business to help children that are behind academically to meet state requirements. You just don't know the number of children even in middle school who can't read well. There are so many children that need academic help today and it's more than foster children. Being a substitute teacher, I have had to give out so many hugs to children whose families are intact. The parents don't have time to interact with them, so they are missing out on the love and attention they need at home. If you could find a way to just help one, God will smile. If you have the knowledge, time, talent or finances and you're not helping someone else, what good are you in God's Kingdom? When I started subbing, I saw a great need where I was. The children's behavior was off the chain and they had no desire to learn. I saw this and I wanted to make a difference. This was around 2005. I felt that if I did something to make things better in the children's lives and they got to know me, I could make a difference. I was already working as a sub for a school system. I wrote the principals, of the elementary and middle school, a letter explaining a program I wanted to do with the children and got no response. You have to have a background check if you're going to be working with children and I'm sure this is everywhere. For several weeks, I heard nothing about my proposal. Then, I start receiving phone calls from someone who worked at the Department of Human Resources. The person wanted to know what my plans were with the children and I explained to her that I was a therapeutic foster parent and a substitute teacher. I explained to her that I wanted to get to know the children and involve them in an opportunity to earn money and teach them entrepreneurial skills. I told her that it was an alternative to the children selling drugs and a way I could help the school manage some of the awful behaviors being exhibited. I felt I could help because by working with them outside the classroom, I could establish a good rapport with a lot of the children. I told her I had worked for the Federal government for 26 years and have been vetted, worked for a local bank for 4 years and have been vetted and that I was a foster parent since 1998 and had been vetted and was working for the school system that turned in the complaint and had been vetted. Once I told the social worker what I was trying to do, I never heard from her again. I don't know which principal turned in the complaint, but I continued to work with them at that time. They are always saying they want community involvement, but when you try to do things to help out situations, they close the door in your face. I have so many more options and opportunities to help other places. I'm just waiting on God to open the doors. I'm saying to you, the children in the classroom and the teachers won't be your problem, the people in the administrative offices will probably be your greatest challenge, especially if they have their favorites. If your days start being taken and given to people who are favored, don't let it deter you, just move on to a place or system that is fair. If you can deal with getting up, getting dressed and going to the school to find out the principal gave away a class you were looking forward to being in and were personally asked by the teacher to do, and gave the assignment to one of her old time favorites, you will have to find your own way to deal with that. My way to deal with it was to go back home because I had another business that I could be taking care of. Favoritism isn't fair, but it does exist.

I am a no-nonsense substitute teacher. I don't play with children because I know they will take advantage of you if they think you are nice. I tell them that if I continue to have behavior problems with them, I will write them up or send them to the office. If you don't have control of the classroom, you will have several students doing things that will make your day miserable and prevent other students from learning. You have to address behavior issues. Since the behaviors were so horrible in schools, I had to come up with a plan for myself. Either, I was going to have a bad day or the students causing the problems would have a bad day. I decided that the students causing the problems would be the ones to have a bad day; therefore, I began to continually write them up with proper cause. As I kept writing them up and they realized I meant business, things began to change with the help of the assistant principal. Other teachers would pass by and my students would be quiet. One of the teachers wanted to know how I kept my classes quiet all day. Another teacher entered the conversation and told her that I had to be threatening the students and told the principal. I told the teacher that I never threaten the students; I made them a promise that if I continued to have to deal with them acting out, I would write them up for disciplinary action and I kept my promise. The principal on one occasion had a staff member to come in and monitor the class. The staff member told me she was coming to monitor one of the students in the next class. But, I knew she was there to monitor me because one of the students had told the principal that I kept writing her up because I didn't like her. But instead of the principal coming to me to discuss the situation with me, she acted on what the student had said which wasn't the truth. I was getting good results and other teachers started calling on me to sub for them. One teacher said she wanted me because one of the other subs played with the children when he was there and upon her return, she would have to get their behaviors under control before she could teach them. I understood exactly what she was saying, because I understand behavior problems from working with foster children. Of course, he was one of the principal's favorites. I could have confronted the principal about the things she was doing as a power play and her need to feel in charge. But I felt the principal had every right to run her school the way she wanted. I could have confronted her about giving my class to someone she referred to as one of their old standbys. That sub hadn't been there since school had started and I was showing up nearly everyday. So, I felt a little unappreciated even though one of the teachers beg me not to stop subbing for them. She said they couldn't get anybody to come there to relieve them. I understood why, I apologized to her I couldn't work for someone like her principal. She would do things to make my life miserable just to show she was boss. I never had a problem with her being boss because I showed up to work and to do a job. It was like there was something about me, she didn't like and I never knew what it was. I don't work where I'm unfairly treated. I prefer to work where I am appreciated. Sometimes they will treat you any kind of way if they feel you need the job. I don't think that is the right attitude. I don't have any desire to sub again because it's not my passion, but if I did do it again, I would choose a city that had the sub finder system where I wouldn't experience the same administrative problems I encountered. Substitute teaching is fun if you can command the respect of the children and the way you do that is to not put up with their nonsense. It's like pushing buttons in foster care. You can't do a good job from sitting at the desk. You will have to be mobile and move around the classroom, standing behind them, standing over them or beside them. They do their most mischievous acts when your back is turned. They make noises when you're facing them. You don't really know who is making the noise and the student knows this. My remedy for that is, after you listen to hear where you think the noise is coming from, pull you up a chair and put it where you are hearing the sound, then take a seat. Sit for several minutes and then stand, remaining in that area. They will usually get tired of you being in their area and they'll stop making the sound. You warn them that if you detect who is keeping up the noise and disrupting the class, you will write them up or send them to the office. The kids' game is to drive the subs away. You have to make up your mind that you won't allow a child or bunch of children to run you off; because they think it's cute and funny. They brag about driving away the subs. I've heard them laugh about it. When I heard them laugh and discuss it in front of me, it became my challenge not to allow the children to drive me away. There are lot of advantages to becoming a substitute teacher, respectfully addressed here as a "Sub" which is the short name. The job is great for men and women who need to earn extra money. You can even make it a full-time profession. Some of the advantages are listed below:

- You have flexible hours and regular work.
- The pay can be good.
- It's a great way to find out if you want to be a future teacher.
- It's easy to become a substitute.
- You'll have many opportunities to exhibit your creative abilities
- You can choose assignments at elementary, middle, or high schools.
- No teaching experience necessary.
- Your earnings can be used as a second income.
- Good substitute teachers are in demand.
- You can continue your education by adjusting your work schedule.
- You can decline any assignment at your discretion.
- Offers a chance to work with today's youth.

Substituting is a six to seven hour a day job. It's not at all like foster care, 24/7. You see, at the end of the day, a substitute teacher can go home and leave the position at school. They don't take assignment papers home to grade. They don't have to make lesson plans for the next day. That's why I was able to do both, a foster parent and a substitute teacher, and still be my own boss, deciding where and for whom I would work for that day. The positions can be a stepping-stone to greater things you want to do in your life. What's the hold up? Call your district Board of Education and find out what it will take for you to start subbing today. My greatest blessings have come in things I didn't want to do or thought I didn't want to do.

A SUBSTITUTE TEACHER'S DAY

A substitute's day begins early, usually around 6:00 AM. If you don't already have your assignment, you might be asked over the telephone. I normally prepare ahead of time whether I'm scheduled already or not. I try to dress professionally, in my nicest clothes, making sure I don't overdress. If I get my assignment by telephone, I would ask the teacher how she wanted me to handle behavior problems and which of the students I could count on to be a helper. All this information is helpful.

The first stop after arriving early at school is the main office to sign in and pick up the items from the teacher's mailbox that you're filling in for. Ask for directions to the teacher's classroom. Lock the door when you get there. Look for the substitute folder with daily instructions in it. Look for emergency procedures for the school in case you have a drill or real emergency, so you will know what to do. The teachers usually have a partnership with one of the teachers next door or across the hall. You can ask them for help. They are always happy to pitch in. You can ask them about the exit route you would take if there were an emergency or drill. I always wrote down the names of the children in the classroom during roll call for each class. If you have to leave the classroom for a drill or emergency, you need to account for the students in your classroom. You're like mother and need to know where your children are at all times. Just simply jot down information as you go along, in case something comes up. After getting settled in the absent teacher's room and going over important procedures, the first thing you need to do after the tardy bell rings is call the roll. Usually if a student comes in late, they have to have a pass from the main office. At the very first encounter of unacceptable behavior, address it then and let them know what is expected of them in the absence of their teacher. Tell them of the consequences of bad behavior. The teacher will sometimes leave instructions for bad behavior. But if the behavior is severe enough, you can send the student to the office. If you haven't been with the students long enough for them to know you and how you operate, you might have to command respect by sending them out or writing them up after warning them and not getting good results. Always exhaust every creative method you can before sending them to the office, unless the office tells you to just send them to them. Find ways to keep them occupied and busy. You have to be creative to come up with what you need. It's good if it is something they're already working on. As in every area of life, you'll have good days and bad days.

MAKING READY FOR THE CHALLENGE

A substitute teacher must make the preparation for a challenge each day. One of the sub's main responsibilities is keeping control of the classroom. Everyday won't be the same. It depends on the class and type of students you're dealing with. Some students will attempt to push your buttons in every way they can. If you let down your guard at any time, some students will take advantage of you. Always be professional in the way you dress and speak. Don't tell them you don't know the answer to the questions they ask. Throw the ball back in their court. Ask them what they think the answer is. Make them think for themselves by asking them questions about what they asked or you ask another student's opinion. Get a debate going on it and possibly make a homeroom assignment out of it. If you get stuck, create an avenue for your way out of it, and always leave the teacher a note so that the student can get the answer he/she is looking for. They'll wonder how did they get to the point where they are and will probably not ask another question to avoid having to engage in coming up with the answer. You can also tell them to find the answer in the book or encourage them to go on to the next question.

Some of today's children have been told that because of their religion, they don't have to stand and participate in the Pledge of Allegiance; so don't force them to participate. It probably would be better for you not to force participation. Familiarize yourself with as many school procedures as you can or get help from the teachers next door. Most teachers are happy you are there and they are glad to help you.

Coffee and beverages are enemies in a sense to the substitute. Indulgence in these possible addictions could cause you to need a restroom break. Sometimes, it will be hours before you are able to use the restroom or arrange for a break. Liquids beware.

Always have some busy work for students in case you come in at a time when the teacher didn't expect to have to be absent. The children will drive you up the walls if they have nothing to do. They will focus on asking you all kinds of questions. They won't stay in their seats or they'll raise their chatter to an unacceptable noise level. I always had something for them to do for fun and for disciplining. Activities like word search puzzles, dot-to-dot activity sheets and crossword puzzles. They all come in handy. If they are old enough to write stories, have them read a book and make a report on it. If you have time, they will love to read it to you. Do whatever is age appropriate for them, like writing essays on topics you give them. You need to do anything that will consume the amount of time you have to spend with them.

Always be prepared with the materials you need before the class begins. You should always have a bag of goodies with you in the event you run out of material. Bring with you a #2 pencil or mechanical pencil to use when you call the roll. It's always good to have a red writing pen and your own paper to make notes on. I would always take my whistle with me in case I couldn't get the students attention. Sometimes, when the whole class is out of order and loud, it took a whistle, travelling over all the voices, to get their attention.

There are things you should be aware of during the class period. Always be aware of what's going on with your students, in the class and outside the classroom. They will get in trouble when you allow them to go to the bathroom. They will be dishonest to get out of the class. They'll tell you that another teacher wants to use them.

You need to follow up on this or tell them to take their seat and if the other teacher sends for them, they will be able to go. They will find any excuse to get up out of their seats. You must speak to them about their behavior and consequences early in the day or early in the period. Don't smile or play with the students. When you smile, make sure you have control over the classroom or they will try to take advantage of you.

Always follow the rules of the school and the classroom. The children will tell you what the teacher allows in the classroom. Sometimes, there will be conflicting viewpoints among the students on what the teacher allows. You have to use your own judgement in these instances.

I have had on several occasions, students that go to sleep in class. I have never thought it a good idea to wake them. If you wake them, you're asking for trouble. The only thing they will do is cause disruption in the class and you don't want that.

You can't control what is going on in the classroom from your seat at the desk. You need to get plenty of rest the night before and eat a good breakfast and be ready to stand and walk down potential problems. The students need to know that your eyes are on them to enforce the rules of behavior you've laid out for them. Sometimes you have to stare them down when you know they are out of order. Most of the time, they will bow their head, hoping you won't be looking at them when they raise their head again. But you should be looking at them just briefly and long enough that they would understand that you know what they're doing. Remember this takes energy and you won't have it if you don't eat breakfast and/or lunch to stay powered up.

You can't ignore students who cause problems in the classroom. You have to keep your eyes on them and call them out when they do wrong. You need to fill out a discipline referral or send them to the office if they continue to disrupt.

You have nearly made the day. Now there are a few more things you need to do before you checkout. You should have the students clean up the area where they sit and allow some to sweep the floor and pick up trash. Leave a note for the teacher describing any incident that might have occurred and need an explanation. Give a list of names of students misbehaving or any students that left the classroom with or without permission.

The information I have provided for you isn't considered law. These are just conventional ways of doing things that I have gained the knowledge through experience and reading. I believe in incorporating ideas and methods that work for me. You should find out what works best for you. You want to enjoy the experience, so you need to know what it will take to accomplish this.

Once again, I have shared the information and knowledge to assist you in gaining income for your families. You have to pursue the necessary avenues to obtain these positions. Are you willing to try? What's more important to you? Will you sit back and expect something to come to you? What are you willing to give? You can make preparations now to provide for your family. The foster care training is free in most places. The substitute teacher position can cost from $50-$100 depending on where you are, but it will be worth it. To obtain a license for substitute teacher should take about two months. There is normally 6 to 10 weeks of training for therapeutic foster care. You would need to check on traditional foster care. It depends on what state you're in. Whichever you choose, be the best you can be and take control of your life. God will reward you for helping his children. Be blessed!

BOTH JOBS PROPELLED
ME FORWARD

During the period of my life while I was fostering and subbing, I didn't feel like anything was going right. I didn't have a working knowledge of the information I have shared with you. It took years of learning and following the Holy Spirit just to get help to make it through. Before I started foster care, I had to have a physical, at which time I was told I had an enlarged heart. I was told I had to immediately begin a regimen of blood pressure medication. I was told I would have to be on blood pressure medication for the rest of my life. The enlarged heart came from working on a stressful government job. I retired from that job at the age of 50. I didn't know how close I was to having a stroke or heart attack until I left. Since I chose to retire when I did, I took a 2% loss on my pension. Fostering and my pension was all I had to live on and sometimes I wouldn't have a child and that was a lost for a period of time. You can't depend on just foster care to make it, but the reimbursements will help you make ends meet. I was always having some financial difficulties and it got to the point where I couldn't afford my medication. Every time my pension increased, my health insurance premiums would increase and also the co-pay for visits to the doctor and the two mediations I was on. Right now I'm paying an insurance premium, but I can't afford to pay the co-pay for the doctor's visit or medicine. I made up my mind 8 years ago to trust God to take care of me and I stop worrying about getting the medication. I go to the doctor to continue to be certified to do foster care, but otherwise, I can't worry about it. I'm struggling to pay a house note that is almost my whole pension. So, you know that the foster care payments help. I tell my agency that I'm not in this just for the money, but without the money I couldn't afford to do it. I sincerely want to help promote good outcomes in the lives of children. But I had to learn how to manage the children without taking on excess stress. In 2000, I went to work for a bank that after 4 years merged with another bank. Here again, came extreme stress and pressure that I couldn't endure. The workload that was placed on me was overwhelming and I had to let that job go. In 2005, I found out that with just a high school education, I could become a substitute teacher. I did and I became good at it after I made the decision to not allow the children to rule my world. I would have probably continued had not the people in authority started being unfair. But God had a greater purpose for me. In the year 2000, I had also tried to start a business to raise funds for foster children. I organized and coordinated a game called Bingo-For-Prizes. This became a fundraiser to raise money to help foster children. I learned how to plan and organize the event, order bingo cards, prizes and tickets for the games. It was family-oriented and all that attended really enjoyed themselves. I did enough of those to learn how I could make it work better. The business failed, but people still ask me why we're not doing the games anymore. During this period, I also gained experience planning and organizing gospel concerts at the church I attended. I partnered with the church and they received 50% of the proceeds. The Holy Spirit has been showing me, teaching me, helping me, storing information for me and reminding me of things He has already taught me. There is no way I could make it without Him and I'm so grateful that He helps me to allow Him to control my life. I am being processed everyday and I love the work. He never leaves me or forsakes me. Thank God!

In, November 2009, we discovered that my mother had progressive dementia. After having to rush over to my mother's home one evening, we learned that she could no longer live alone. We were concerned and didn't want my mother in a nursing home for all the obvious reasons. No one could care for her the way we could. We talked to her medical doctor and told him we didn't want to put my mother in a nursing home. It just so happened that her doctor was over the hospice program in Alabama. He immediately arranged for the hospice people to come out and talk to me. No, it had nothing to do with death panels. They accepted my mother into the program and the nurse came out to see her once a week and someone came everyday to give her a bath and change the linen. She was furnished whatever type of equipment she needed. Of course, you know I had to give up my job substituting for nearly a year to become a caregiver, but I could still do foster care. My mother lived nine months and a few days before she succumbed to that dreadful disease. The foster child that I had at the time, did everything he could to help me with my mother. He'd rub her face, sit with her, go and get me whatever I needed for her and try to help feed her. He would help me get my mother from the sofa to her wheelchair, taking her back and forth to bed and the den to watch television. He finally got to go live with his father, which he wanted more than anything in the world. Before he left, he asked me to let him know if something happened to Grandma. I called him when my mother passed and he expressed that he wanted to go to her funeral. I told him to get permission from his Dad and I would send my oldest daughter to pick him up. He was the first child that I ever saw genuinely having emotions for someone else. He called me for a period of time afterward, and I had his stepmother's cell phone number to reach him, but the number was changed. I live in hope that all is well with him and I feel if he ever need me, he'll call me and I'll be there for him.

In 2008, I started watching politics on television. It seems as though we would have a chance to make history. I learned that Barack Obama worked as a community organizer. He often talked about community service, at least that's what I was hearing and I realized that it was something I wanted to accomplish in my life. But bringing people together in unity seemed the most difficult thing in the world to do. People don't seem to want to hear about unity or practice coming together to do anything. They want to do things their way, which fails more often than not. After having had a failed business, I wanted to try again. I thought up a name I wanted to use. I wanted to involve my family. The Holy Spirit brought to my memory some instructions that I heard from several ministers. One was, write the vision down. So, I had my son find a host for my website. I decided the name of my business would be Community Families United Network, Inc. I did what was necessary to register my business as a nonprofit with the State of Alabama. I wrote the information I wanted on my site and gave it to my son who is a site builder and he took it from there. I googled up community service organizations and stumbled upon Corporation for National & Community Service. I was looking for information on how to get help to become a nonprofit organization. I was referred to another agency in Montgomery, Alabama who referred me to a nonprofit law clinic in Alabama. I was led through the process of filling a 1023 application to receive a determination of nonprofit status. I also had to write the bylaws to file with the state, along with the articles of incorporation. The attorney that helped me said that I would be able to help foster children with what my objectives and goals are. I didn't have the money to pay the fee to file the 1023 and God blessed me with a $1700 check to get the job done. The fee is only $850 and now I'm waiting on the determination letter.

Before I could get the 1023 application done, I was prompted to work on a book that I started writing in 2003. I didn't have the money to publish the book, approximately $2500. I was amazed to be lead to a Print On Demand (POD) self-publishing website. I self-published my book called "Following The Millennial Christ" a nonfiction book about a member of my family and me being processed to live in the Kingdom. The most dreadful part of publishing a book to me is editing it. That means you have to read the book over and over again to find mistakes and correct them. It is really tiresome. But it saves you a lot of money if you do it yourself. I am very pleased with the outcome. I can't say that it's not hard work at first. But this is my second book and I've learned how to make this one turn out all better. The first one had about ten revisions and I learned from it and my son who also helped me.

I had to write the objectives and purpose of my company to be posted to the website and they are as listed.

OBJECTIVES & PURPOSES

The primary objectives and purposes of this corporation shall be"

- To foster and nurture relationships of children in foster care, low-income families and at risk youth in the community by providing a Children Support Group with adult supervision, to address children issues, offer character building training, life and social learning skills, entrepreneurial skills, taught by facilitators and through the access of computers, monitored Internet curriculums and other multi-media educational resources, to help prepare young individuals for life and produce great citizens. To hold these meetings at faith-based facilities where children can form a connection and friendship to other families who will lend their encouragement and support.
- To provide grades K-3 an after school and summer program to help raise the level of literacy through academic enrichment and character building. To involve volunteer literacy aids and student peer helpers in training and improving literacy levels. To assist schools and PTA/PTO organizations in

raising funds for supplies and other needs to promote literacy excellence.

- To provide counselling, social and financial help to those in foster care, who are aging out of the system or have already, aged out; to help them become inclusive and acceptable in a larger society. To provide a case manager to oversee the management and care of each of these youth, working to provide community family support for these individuals by establishing and maintaining a connection and base for them to come to, thereby increasing the possibilities for them to become stable and responsible adult citizens.

- To provide a community-based Parent Support Group for the purpose of learning parenting skills and fostering better communication, offering a non-judgmental atmosphere for discussions and provide educational opportunities, all in the spirit of fun.

- To sponsor programs to reward and exhibit the growth, talents and abilities of students in the network, thereby inspiring and encouraging others to continue to strive for success.

- To encourage, promote and include volunteers in all aspects of our community service efforts, finding and implementing programs to recruit and retain good volunteers.

- To give individuals access to a social networking tool on our interactive website where they will be able to blog, share and express themselves in various forums.

- To sponsor special events involving public performance by the corporation's performance troupe, as well by other community performing art groups for the purpose of supporting the goals and objectives of the corporation.

- To sponsor a weekly program on public television, highlighting positive community, school and local events.

The attorney also had me to write the narrative for my company. This is something I've never done before either.

So, I looked for documents that contained summaries over the Internet and received so much information that helped me pull my narrative together. A summarization of the narrative was used in compiling the information for the 1023 application.

NARRATIVE

Community Families United Network Inc. (CFUN) is an organization that seeks to provide social and educational services to families and communities. CFUN is located at 466 Second Street, North in Birmingham, Alabama. CFUN carries out its activities at this office, public schools, community centers, public meeting facilities and churches located in Birmingham and surrounding cities. CFUN has been incorporated since September 4, 2008.

CFUN engages in instructional, educational and performance driven activities targeted for low-income, foster and at-risk youth, not excluding adults who are in need. Current activities include rounding up community talent to participate in our entrepreneurial program for young people that will help finance the objectives of the organization. Another activity is to expand an after-school academic enrichment program for grades K-3 to improve literacy among youth. The implementation of this program was the summer of 2009 with ten students. CFUN has additional plans to institute a "Life Skills Learning" program for children, separate community-based support groups for parents and youth. CFUN is also providing an interactive website for the purpose of communication and heartfelt expressions to unite supporters and bring communities together. CFUN will sponsor special events involving public performances of supporters of the organization and communities to support the goals and objectives of the network.

All of CFUN's activities serve three fundamental purposes. First, the activities promote social welfare, second, they promote literacy and third, they promote the Arts & Entertainment. All purposes lessen the burdens of the government by combating juvenile delinquency and community deterioration while enhancing the happiness and well being of community members.

Promotion of Social Welfare

CFUN plays a significant role in the promotion of social welfare for children. The majority of the children are from lower economic families in areas of cities where children are prone to violence a illiteracy. CFUN's activities will keep children off the streets by engaging them in skills training and creative arts. CFUN provides an Internet-based learning curriculum, which enhances the learning ability of children by capturing their minds through visual media that makes learning fun. Currently, approximately 80% of CFUN's resources are spent on event planning and organizing. The additional 20% is allocated toward enrichment and character building supplies. In the upcoming year, CFUN plans to roll out an apprenticeship/job skill-training program with the help of mentors that will volunteer their time to teach.

CFUN is in the process of offering fundraising services to schools to help with their projects because of excessive cuts in budgets. CFUN, through the service given schools, has developed an income-earning program for young people to learn how to be online processors. Each school will have one student representative. Youth will receive free entrepreneurial training provided by qualified instructions and receive practical experience as an ordering agent.

CFUN's objective is to work with foster children and their families to help children feel inclusive in a greater community. The focus will be to extend them a hand up and not just a hand out. CFUN will provide a support base of believers to mentor children by showing a sincere interest in their success; tutor children to help them excel academically and to support and build emotional stability in children by giving them unconditional love and support that would ordinarily be expected to come from their biological family. CFUN will use the "Village" concept to seek ways to create opportunities for all our children and encourage them to attain the highest education possible. CFUN will provide a licensed case manage to resolve youth problems. As CFUN continue to grow, its activities will be to add caring people to the staff to assist youth with problems pertaining to housing, education, life skills and independent living.

Promotion of Literacy

World Literacy Facts states that over 780 million adults in the world are illiterate. 64% of the world's illiterate are women. Nearly 60 per cent of the estimated 113 million children who do not attend primary school worldwide are girls. On average, nearly one in three children does not complete 5 years of primary education, the minimum required for acquiring basic literacy. CFUN is providing academic enrichment to school children having difficulty in important subjects; those who have fallen behind and need intensive help to meet state requirements in basic comprehensive subjects and those students who want to advance above their required level of learning in grades K-3. CFUN is using and will use peer helpers and tutors to assist and address the educational needs after making an assessment for each participant.

In the program year, 2009-2010, in addition to the academic enrichment program launched for grades K-3, CFUN will implement a Life Skills Training component for middle school youth participants by beginning a video program that will teach character building and basic living skills for youth. CFUN will establish a Children Support Network to discuss children issues, exhibit and exchange caring attitudes, show kindness, express encouragement, motivate and build self-confidence in every child.

Promotion of the Arts & Entertainment

Aside from CFUN's purpose of promoting social welfare and education, its activities will clearly engage in the Arts & Entertainment.

CFUN's objective is to find seriously talented individuals, adults and children, in the community to showcase their talent to bring them recognition and build our communities. Arts & Entertainment will provide some of the funding of CFUN's programs and its kid's entrepreneurial project. It will provide inspiration and incentive so that others will actively engage in the activities. CFUN will promote talent if it is worthy by assisting in launching careers or providing information where talented individuals can further their interests. The Arts & Entertainment can help nurture talent and can be an important part of growth in an individual's future and will provide to help find a viable option for future endeavors. CFUN will obtain television time on the public access stations to display community talent at sponsored events. CFUN is working on getting a 1-hour weekly spot on public access television. The events will be video-graphed and shown on a weekly program. This television access will be used to bring communities, schools and parents together in a positive way to show a positive outcome, which communities will learn how to deal with similar problems by sharing ideas and coming together in unity to solve them.

Future Plans

CFUN plans to expand its academic enrichment program to include more children. Also, to convince faith-based organizations to have satellite enrichment program at their facilities. CFUN will expand the growth of supporters to surrounding cities and neighboring states. Another future activity of CFUN will be to build a recreation fun place for its supporters that will supply numerous jobs for people in the community and help promote academic achievement for students.

I truly hope you can read and understand how both positions, foster parent and substitute teacher, have propelled me into a greater and larger purpose in God. I am so excited about my future and helping children and adults become successful. There is such a need in raising the standards of our families, especially our children. I think the kindest thing one can do is to feed a child food and knowledge that will sustain him/her for a lifetime. The needs of children are great everywhere today. What can we do as a "village" to help the masses? In life, we're only given a certain amount of time and most of us squander it and never find God's purpose for our lives. Please read the information carefully and consider it prayerfully, and then set out to create and build you a career promoting children and education today. God is smiling!

A Work-In-Progress

I am presently working my plan for my business. I am figuring out ways to provide income-earning opportunities for families everywhere. I am working to bring people together to have them involved in my program. I am trying to partner with schools to raise money for them and to start preparing for my academic enrichment program for grades K-3 while I wait for my determination. I've made a lifetime commitment to help the people of Haiti with some of the proceeds from the sale of my book. I am reaching out to churches to see if they will help my organization in any way. I am finding out how very hard it is to get the church involved in helping the poor. I have written guidelines that consist of 14 pages to provide instructions for those that will work with us independent contractors. We need event planners/coordinators to help us raise money for public schools. My prayer of faith is that God will speak to the hearts of the people to move in His direction to open doors to help people in need, thereby helping themselves in their endeavors. So, dismiss the fear you have. Get involved, accept rejection, move on and help children today. Represent God and do it well. Don't hold back on your love for others. Show it to people everyday and everywhere. I am turning this book over to God to handle, as He will. For, only He can change the hearts of mankind. I wrote the following letter to 9 different pastors of churches in Birmingham.

May 3, 2009

Dear Pastor:

Community Families United Network, Inc. (CFUN) is a newly incorporated business in the City of Birmingham. We are not housed in a building yet, but hope to be very soon. We are launching a pre-emptive strike against a very dismal outlook of our economic future. We are concerned about our families and communities. We believe that there is "Power In The People". Unity is such a difficult task to achieve, especially during thriving times. **NOW** is a time of crisis and it is time for us to take a proactive approach to change the severity of expected conditions. We must be like ants, making preparation for what is to come, **NOW!** We know that lack in the lives of people increases the opportunity for more crime in our communities and more burdens for those who are less fortunate than others. Times are so critical and we can't sit by passively, waiting for something bad or good to happen. We must engage as ordinary citizens to make a difference for our children and our communities.

CFUN goals include an outreach to help children in foster care, low-income families and youth at risk. Our compassionate plea to you as a pastor is to support our grassroots advocacy for families and communities. You can help us by:

- Providing your congregation with our website address, **www. communityfamilyunitednetwork.org**. It is an interactive website. They can register and immediately become a partner for change. Please encourage your congregation to register. There is no registration fee, but lots of opportunities to assist.
- Provide a meeting place for a parent support group to discuss youth and other issues.
- Provide a meeting place for a children support group. Our objective is to provide entrepreneurial training, life skills

training, and character building, along with discussing children issues.

- We need good, committed volunteers, so, please encourage your congregation to consider volunteering. They can sign up on our website.
- We hope you will loan us your musicians, choirs, soloists, praise dancers and other talent to help us with the entertainment portion of our endeavor. This is one of the ways we will fund our events and provide a way for youth to practice their entrepreneurial skills to become productive, responsible citizens.

My prayer is that God will bless you and your congregation. Please prayerfully consider assisting us in whatever way you can with this project. Let us hear from you, soon!

Sincerely,

Lois Simmons, President CFUN

To this day, I have received no response of any type from any of these pastors. This disturbed me for a while. After many months, my response was this:

A Sobering Message to Middle Class Americans...

I grew up in low-income neighborhoods most of my life. I have always had a desire to help others. I haven't attained middle class status, yet and my needs are being met daily. If you came through near poverty to arrive at a middle class status today, then how can you forget the poor you left behind? This year I started building a business to assist families and communities with problems they are having in education and finances. Our main focus will be on instilling a sense of great citizenship in our school-age youth through education, character building and by setting good examples as responsible adults. Realizing I couldn't accomplish my dream alone, I decided to reach out to pastors and leaders of faith-based organizations. I wrote nine churches in Birmingham, Alabama four months ago inviting them to join with me in working to ease the burdens of families by creating income earning opportunities for our youth and teaching them entrepreneurial skills to help them become self-sufficient in the future. I didn't ask these organizations for any money. I asked them to make our organization known to members of their congregation by inviting them to our website. I asked them to encourage their members to volunteer to help with support groups for parents and youth issues. And to this date, I haven't heard from any of the nine churches that I corresponded to. If you can't go to the church for help, to whom do you turn? It's frightening to think that during these serious economic times, the doors of the churches are closed. Middle class Americans are in crisis. Can you imagine the state of the poor in this nation? If the pastors of great churches have their own agenda and won't open the doors to the poor, whom are they representing in their lavish buildings? They've turned their backs on the poor, but will they treat the middle class the same when they've suffered loss or fallen on hard times. Do they feel the church building is too nice for the poor to enter in? Visit us on the web at www.MyCfun.org.

I am grateful for the opportunity to share portions of my life with you and I hope you use the information to propel yourself to somewhere you want to go. Depend on God only. Man will disappoint you most of the time. You are eternally blessed!